I0813163

DISCOVERING THE UNITED STATES

New Hampshire

BY CHRISTY MIHALY

abdobooks.com

Printed in China.
052024
092024

Cover Photo: Shutterstock Images
Interior Photos: Jerry Gantar/Shutterstock Images, 4–5; Dave Alan/E+/Getty Images, 6 (top left); Alex Ugalek/Shutterstock Images, 6 (top right); Shutterstock Images, 6 (bottom left), 10; Phil Degginger/Alamy, 6 (bottom right); Denis Tangney Jr./iStockphoto, 9; Ellen McKnight/Alamy, 12–13; Lewis Wickes Hine/Library of Congress/VCG/Corbis Historical/Getty Images, 15; John Greim/LightRocket/Getty Images, 17; Viktor Cvetkovic/iStockphoto, 18; iStockphoto, 20–21, 28 (top right); Jason Heid/iStockphoto, 22; Jeffrey M. Frank/Shutterstock Images, 25; Alizada Studios/Shutterstock Images, 26; Red Line Editorial, 28 (top left), 29; EcoPhotography.com/Alamy, 28 (bottom left); Grindstone Media Group/Shutterstock Images, 28 (bottom right)

Editor: Christa Kelly
Series Designer: Katharine Hale

Library of Congress Control Number: 2023949335

Publisher's Cataloging-in-Publication Data

Names: Mihaly, Christy, author.
Title: New Hampshire / by Christy Mihaly
Description: Minneapolis, Minnesota: Abdo Publishing, 2025 | Series: Discovering the United States | Includes online resources and index.
Identifiers: ISBN 9781098293994 (lib. bdg.) | ISBN 9798384913269 (ebook)
Subjects: LCSH: U.S. states--Juvenile literature. | New Hampshire--History--Juvenile literature. | Northeastern States--Juvenile literature. | Physical geography--United States--Juvenile literature.
Classification: DDC 973--dc23

All population data taken from:
"Estimates of Population by Sex, Race, and Hispanic Origin: April 1, 2020 to July 1, 2022." *US Census Bureau, Population Division,* June 2023, census.gov.

CONTENTS

CHAPTER 1
The Town of Hill 4

CHAPTER 2
The People of New Hampshire 12

CHAPTER 3
Places in New Hampshire 20

State Map 28
Glossary 30
Online Resources 31
Learn More 31
Index 32
About the Author 32

The town of Hill was forced to move when a dam was built on the Pemigewasset River.

The Town of Hill

In February 1937, bad news arrived in Hill, New Hampshire. The government was building a dam on the nearby river. The dam would raise the water level. Hill would be completely flooded.

Hill was a small town. Only a few hundred people lived there.

New Hampshire Facts

DATE OF STATEHOOD
June 21, 1788

CAPITAL
Concord

POPULATION
1,395,231

AREA
9,349 square miles (24,214 sq km)

STATE BIRD

Purple finch

STATE TREE

White birch

STATE FLOWER

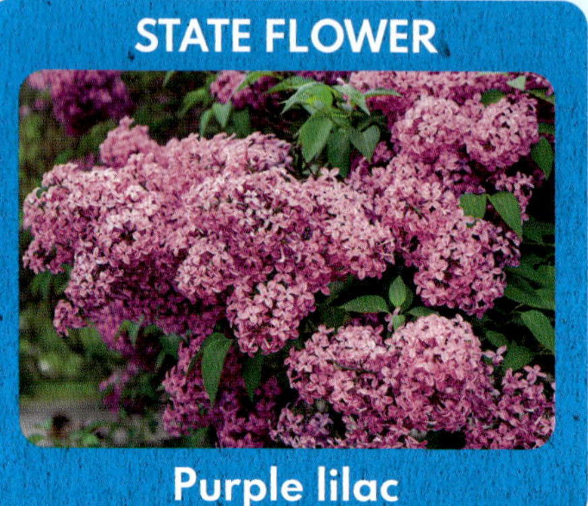

Purple lilac

STATE SPIDER

Daring jumping spider

Each US state has a different population, size, and capital city. States also have state symbols.

The government paid them to leave. The people could have moved to other towns, but they decided to stick together. They bought land on higher ground. They moved 14 of Hill's buildings there. Then they built more.

By 1941, the people of Hill had a new town hall and a school. They had new homes on their new land. The town of Hill lives on today, just up the hill from the old village.

New Hampshire's Land

New Hampshire is in the Northeast region of the United States. Canada borders the state to the north. Vermont lies to the west, separated from New Hampshire by the Connecticut River. Massachusetts is to the south. To the east is Maine.

The Atlantic Ocean borders the southeast corner of New Hampshire. The state's coastline is just 18 miles (29 km) long. That is the shortest coastline of any state.

Northern New Hampshire is home to the White Mountains. These are tall, rocky peaks. The tallest is Mount Washington. Rare plants grow in these mountains. Dwarf cinquefoil is one of these plants. It is a tiny yellow flower that is found only in the White Mountains.

There are about 1,000 lakes and ponds in New Hampshire. Lake Winnipesaukee is

Nicknames

New Hampshire has many nicknames. Some call it the Granite State because of the large amount of granite it has. Others call it the White Mountain State or America's Switzerland. This is because of the state's tall peaks. Still others call it the Mother of Rivers. This name is due to the many rivers that begin in the White Mountains.

The Abenaki Nation calls Mount Washington *Agiocochook*. The name means "Home of the Great Spirit."

the largest. The state also has many rivers. Their total length is more than 10,000 miles (16,000 km).

Many animals call New Hampshire home. Among them are moose, beavers, and snowshoe hares. The state also has many birds such as owls and hawks.

Scientists have a base on the top of Mount Washington.

New Hampshire's Climate

New Hampshire has four seasons. Summers are short and mild. In autumn, leaves turn red and gold before falling from the trees. Winters are long and cold. Plants grow in spring.

The White Mountains have especially harsh weather. They have some of the strongest wind gusts in the world. The winds are often cold. The coldest **wind chill** in US history was measured on Mount Washington in 2023. The temperature was −108.4 degrees Fahrenheit (−78°C).

Further Evidence

Look at the website below. Does it give any new evidence to support Chapter One?

New Hampshire

abdocorelibrary.com/discovering-new-hampshire

Hundreds of years ago, Abenaki people lived in dome-shaped houses called wigwams.

The People of New Hampshire

The first people arrived in New Hampshire at least 10,000 years ago. They were American Indians. They formed nations. These include the Abenaki and Pennacook nations. The Abenaki and Pennacook hunted. They built villages and farmed.

Colony to State

English settlers arrived in 1623. They built two fishing villages on the coast. They traded with the native people. In 1679, the land became the English **colony** of New Hampshire.

By the late 1600s, the number of Abenaki and Pennacook people in New Hampshire was quickly decreasing. Many American Indian people died from European diseases. Others moved to Canada when settlers stole their land.

In January 1776, New Hampshire was the first colony to break away from England. The colonists fought against England in the Revolutionary War (1775—1783). In 1788, New Hampshire joined the United States as the ninth state.

Mill work was dangerous and involved long work hours. Some workers were injured or killed by the machines.

In the 1800s, New Hampshire companies built large **textile mills**. They made cotton and wool cloth. The mills brought many people to the state. **Immigrants** came from Canada and Europe to find work.

Today, about 89 percent of people in New Hampshire are white. Almost 5 percent are Hispanic or Latino. About 3 percent are Asian.

Approximately 2 percent are Black. Less than 0.5 percent are American Indian.

Culture

Food is an important part of culture in New Hampshire. Farmers grow corn, apples, and other crops. Some people fish for trout and salmon. Others hunt deer and

First in the Nation

Since 1920, New Hampshire has held the first primary election of the US presidential race. State primaries are elections among candidates from one political group. The winner of the state primaries becomes that party's candidate. That candidate runs against other parties' candidates in the November election.

New Hampshire's seafood industry brings in $20 million every year.

moose for meat. On the coast, people harvest lobster and clams.

Outdoor activities are also important to people in New Hampshire. In the winter, people ski and snowboard. Some ice skate and snowmobile.

Industries

Many people in New Hampshire work in tourism. They take care of the state's visitors.

New Hampshire adopted a state flag in 1909. The flag features the state seal.

Travelers come to the state to camp, ski, and see historical sites.

Health care is another major **industry** in New Hampshire. Many of the state's universities and hospitals do medical research. They develop products that save lives.

Other people in New Hampshire work in technology. Some produce clean energy. Some make computer parts. Others work on creating new inventions.

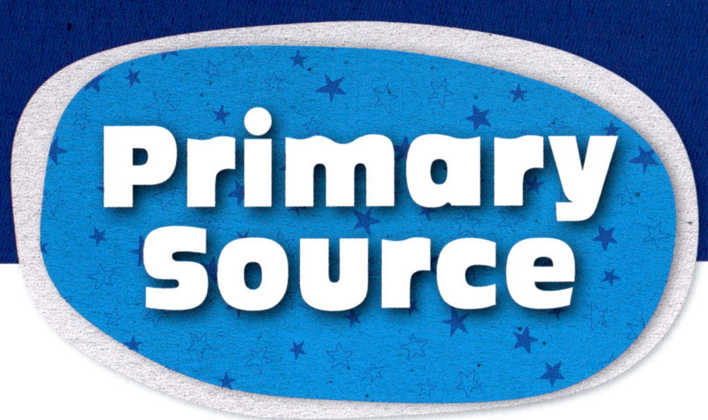

David Souter is from New Hampshire. He joined the US Supreme Court in 1990. He loved returning home. He said:

> The **restoration** comes not only from the landscape and air, though they play their significant part, but from the people. I feel a strong need to be in New Hampshire . . . .

Source: Philip Rucker. "Justice Souter Longs for Rural Hideaway." *Seattle Times*, 3 May 2009. seattletimes.com. Accessed 3 Nov. 2023.

What's the Big Idea?

Read this quote carefully. What is its main idea? Explain how the main idea is supported by details.

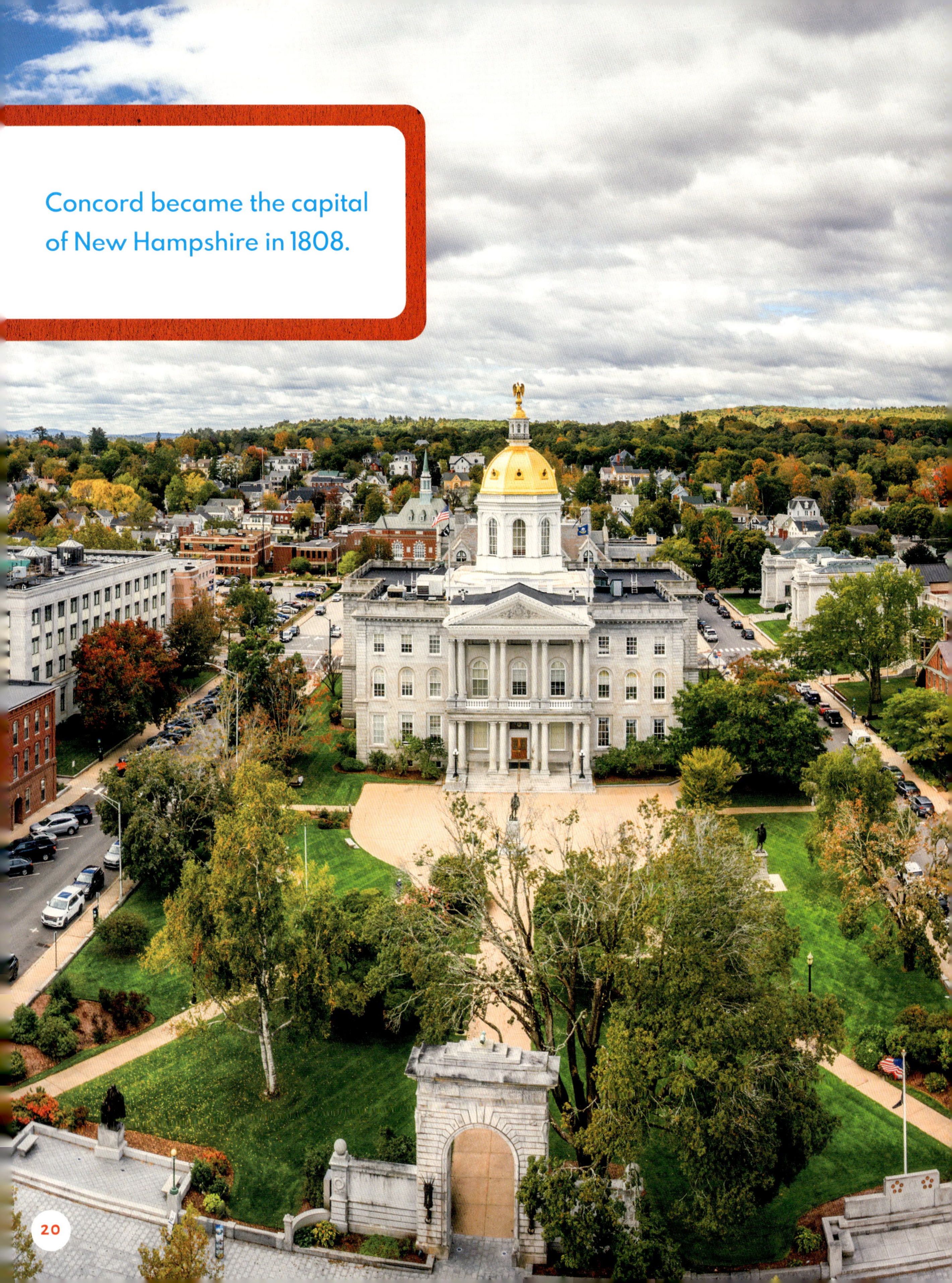

Concord became the capital of New Hampshire in 1808.

CHAPTER 3

Places in New Hampshire

New Hampshire's capital is Concord. It is the third most **populated** city in the state. It is home to the McAuliffe-Shepard Discovery Center. This science museum honors Christa McAuliffe and Alan Shepard, two astronauts from New Hampshire.

Franconia Notch State Park is especially popular in the fall when the leaves change color.

New Hampshire's most populated city is Manchester. The city is home to many colleges. In the 1800s and 1900s, there were many textile mills there. Today, the old mill buildings contain shops and apartments.

Parks

New Hampshire has 76 state parks. One of the state's most popular parks is Franconia Notch State Park. The park is located in the White Mountains. In the summer, visitors can swim and camp. In the winter, they can ski.

Old Man of the Mountain

Cannon Mountain is part of the White Mountains. It was known for its strange rock formation. A piece of the mountain jutted out, forming what looked like a human face. Many people called the formation the Old Man of the Mountain. The Abenaki people called it Stone Face. In 2003, the cliff cracked and collapsed, destroying the rock formation.

Odiorne Point State Park is another popular park. It's located on New Hampshire's coastline. Tourists can hike on the rocky coast. They can also visit the Seacoast Science Center. The center's exhibits teach visitors about ocean **conservation**.

Some tourists come to New Hampshire to see Saint-Gaudens National Historical Park. In 1885, the park's land was home to the sculptor Augustus Saint-Gaudens. Today, the park preserves Saint-Gaudens's house and surrounding gardens.

Landmarks

New Hampshire has several famous landmarks. One such landmark is the Strawbery Banke

Saint-Gaudens National Historical Park is in the town of Cornish.

Museum in Portsmouth. The museum opened in 1965. It teaches visitors about the city's history. It also teaches people about the American Indian Nations who are native to the land.

When the USS *Albacore* was first made, it was the fastest submarine ever built.

Visitors can explore historical buildings. They can also interact with museum guides, many of whom are dressed in historical clothes.

The USS *Albacore* Museum is another popular landmark. The museum is home to the USS *Albacore*, a submarine built in New Hampshire. The US Navy used the submarine from 1953 to 1972. Visitors can tour the submarine.

New Hampshire has many places to explore. Visitors can learn about the state's history. They can see the state's beautiful forests and mountains. New Hampshire offers new and exciting adventures for everyone.

Explore Online

Visit the website below. What information does it give you that was not in Chapter Three?

Sea Coast Science Center

abdocorelibrary.com/discovering-new-hampshire

State Map

KEY

Capital

Park

City or town

Point of interest

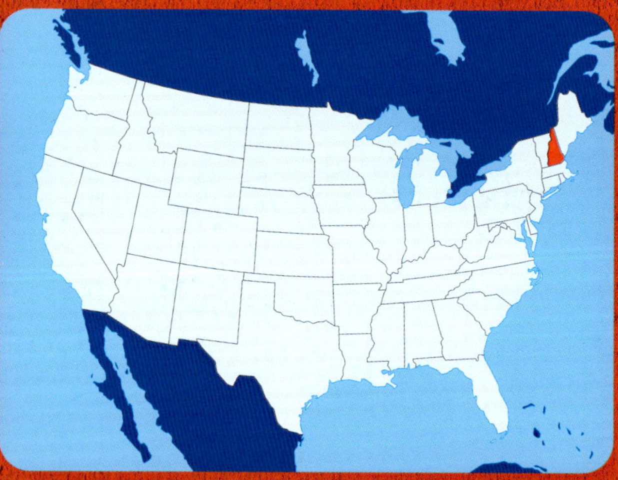

Mount Washington Cog Railway

New Hampshire Motor Speedway

Odiorne Point State Park

New Hampshire: The Granite State

Glossary

colony
an area that is controlled by another country

conservation
the protection of something so it lasts into the future

immigrants
people who move to a different country

industry
a group of businesses that serve similar purposes

populated
settled or lived in

restoration
the process of becoming refreshed

textile mills
factories that produce cloth

wind chill
a measurement in degrees of how cold the air feels given the temperature and the wind speed

Online Resources

To learn more about New Hampshire, visit our free resource websites below.

Visit **abdocorelibrary.com** or scan this QR code for free Common Core resources for teachers and students, including vetted activities, multimedia, and booklinks, for deeper subject comprehension.

Visit **abdobooklinks.com** or scan this QR code for free additional online weblinks for further learning. These links are routinely monitored and updated to provide the most current information available.

Learn More

Knoblock, Teresa M., and Glenn A. Knoblock. *Fighting for Freedom.* Free People, 2022.

London, Martha. *Military Submarines.* Abdo, 2020.

Murray, Julie. *New Hampshire.* Abdo, 2020.

Index

Abenaki nation, 13–14, 23

Cannon Mountain, 23
Concord, 6, 21

Franconia Notch State Park, 23

Hill, 5–7

Manchester, 22
Mount Washington, 8, 11

Odiorne Point State Park, 24

Pennacook nation, 13–14
Portsmouth, 24–26

Revolutionary War, 14

Saint-Gaudens National Historical Park, 24
Strawbery Banke Museum, 24–26

USS *Albacore* Museum, 26–27

White Mountains, 8, 11, 23

About the Author

Christy Mihaly is a children's author and poet. She has written more than 35 books, mostly nonfiction. She went to college in New Hampshire and continues to be a frequent visitor to the Granite State. She now lives across the Connecticut River in Vermont.